Explore the Outdoors

Fishing

Have Fun, Be Smart

by Captain Dane Solomon

Rosen Publishing Group, Inc.
New York

To the people I love the most: Marietta, you are my inspiration; Dad and Mom, without your support I would not be where I am today.

The author would like to thank his grandfathers, Grandpa Mitch and Grandpa Mike. If they had not taken him fishing when he was young, Captain Solomon would not be the knowledgeable fisherman he is today.

Published in 2000 by The Rosen Publishing Group, Inc.
29 East 21st Street, New York, NY 10010

First Edition

Library of Congress Cataloging-in-Publication Data

Solomon, Dane.
Fishing: have fun, be smart / Dane Solomon.
    p. cm. — (Explore the outdoors)
Includes bibliographical references (p.) and index.
Summary: Explains the basics of freshwater and saltwater fishing, including equipment, types of fish to catch, and safety precautions.
    ISBN 0-8239-3168-4
1. Fishing—Juvenile literature. [1. Fishing.] I. Title. II. Series.

SH445.S68 2000
799.1—dc21

                                                  99-059311

Manufactured in the United States of America

Contents

Introduction

Fishing has been around for thousands of years. People began to fish in order to survive and feed their families. If they did not catch fish, they did not eat. Now, however, the majority of people who fish do so for the enjoyment of it, as well as for a little something to eat.

Fishing is a sport that can involve anybody, no matter what size, color, or age the person may be. A person does not need to be born with special athletic talents, an IQ of 150, a body like Arnold's, or the looks of a movie star to be a fisherman. In addition, you don't necessarily have to spend a lot of money on expensive equipment in order to fish, and it's as close as the creek, river, or lake nearest your home.

If you have never been introduced to fishing before and would like to know more about the sport, this book will give you an idea of how to get started. If you've already started fishing, you'll get a good overview of other kinds of fishing you may want to try. Safety is an important part of this sport, too, and you'll learn how to make sure you have a good time without putting yourself at risk of getting hurt.

Fishing is a sport that many people enjoy throughout their lives, and there's no time like the present to get started!

1 Fishing Basics

As you start to get interested in fishing, you will see that there are a wide range of tools available to you. The methods people use to catch fish today are actually very similar to those used thousands of years ago. The difference between catching fish thousands of years ago and catching fish today is not how people catch the fish but which types of materials are used to make the spears, nets, hooks, and fishing line.

Tools—Then and Now

In the past, spears—primarily made of a sharpened piece of wood or bone attached to the end of a pole of some sort—were used to catch fish in shallow waters such as ponds, rivers, and streams. Nets, made from woven materials such

as threads or thin vines, and fish traps were used when there were large numbers of fish in one area of an ocean or bay. Hook and line, a method very popular today, was used by people thousands of years ago as well—hooks were made

How Fish Swim

If you've ever gone swimming, you know that it's much harder to move your body through water than through air. This is because water is denser than air and gives more resistance.

Have you ever wondered how fish seem to move so quickly and gracefully? For starters, their streamlined shape lets fish glide through the water with a minimum of resistance. Fish also excrete a special kind of slime from their skin that helps them travel smoothly through the water. (Having neither a streamlined shape nor—in most cases—special slime, humans are at a great disadvantage when it comes to swimming!)

As a fish swims, it relies on its skeleton for framework, its muscles for power, and its fins for thrust and direction.

of shaped bone or wood, and fishing line was made from animal parts or from thin plant materials such as roots, vines, or certain types of grass.

Today spears are made of stronger materials, such as aluminum or hard plastic. Nets are still woven, but they are woven with stronger, lighter materials. Fishing hooks are made from strong metals, such as steel or bronze, and fishing

Technically Speaking

Fish (n.): Any of a large group of cold-blooded, finned aquatic vertebrates. Fish are generally scaled and breathe by passing water over gills. There are three classes of modern fish:

I. AGNATHA—Primitive jawless fish (lampreys, hagfish)
II. CHONDRICHTHYES—Jawed fish with skeletons made of cartilage (sharks, rays)
III. OSTEICHTHYES—Fish with bony skeletons (trout, bass, salmon)

line is made from a material called monofilament. You'll find out more about the equipment you'll need in order to fish in chapter four.

Why Fish?

Unlike in the past, most people today don't fish out of necessity. Those who fish for a living are called commercial fishermen. Commercial fishermen catch thousands of pounds of fish with nets, traps, hooks, and line to sell to restaurants and people like you and me.

Most fishermen today are sport fishermen. They don't go fishing to sell the fish they catch; they fish for enjoyment—and for the skill, concentration, and knowledge involved. Going out with your family or buddies can be a great way to bond with each other and get closer to nature. And of course, if you do catch something, you can either let it go or bring it home for dinner.

2 Freshwater Fishing

When you decide that fishing is a sport you want to try, freshwater fishing is a great place to start. Although the United States and Canada have beautiful coastal regions and many saltwater spots to fish, most people live too far away to saltwater fish very often. In contrast, you can probably find a freshwater fishing spot close to where you live.

How Can I Tell If a Body of Water Is Freshwater?

There are a few simple ways to tell if the water you are about to fish is freshwater and not saltwater. If you see that the body of water you wish to fish is surrounded by land, most likely the water is freshwater. You can also taste the water to make sure it doesn't taste salty.

Depending on where you live, your favorite fishing spot may be a lake or pond close to your home. The first thing you should look for in a lake or pond is water cleanliness. If you can see to the bottom of the pond or lake, chances are the water is clean enough to hold fish.

Secondly, look for plants or weeds growing in the water. If you do not see any types of plants or weeds in the water, the

water is probably poisoned or polluted, and nothing will be living in it, including fish.

The last thing to look for is signs of animal life, such as frogs, small fish, or even turtles. If you see any signs of animals in the water, chances are good there will be fish to catch. When you find a pond or lake close to home that is clean and has plant and animal life, you have found your fishing spot.

Types of Freshwater Fish

Bass

There are many different kinds of freshwater fish that you can catch in your local freshwater fishing spot. The most common of these fish is the largemouth bass. The large-mouth bass now lives in every state in the continental United States. It can live in small ponds, lakes, and even man-made reservoirs. The biggest largemouth bass caught on a rod and reel to date is twenty-two pounds, four ounces. In the southern part of the United States, largemouth bass can be caught all year round. In the northern part of the United States, such as New York and Michigan, largemouth bass can also be caught all year round, but they are easier to catch from April to October.

Largemouth bass are predators—they will feed on almost anything that is put in front of them. They feed on small fish, frogs, mice, worms, crawfish, and similar critters. To find these fish, find a structure—such as a fallen tree, weeds, or rocks—in the water you are fishing; these places are popular spots for bass to congregate.

Another fish is the smallmouth bass. The small-mouth bass is a more active bass and smaller—the largest smallmouth bass ever caught was about eleven pounds. It is a

member of the sunfish family and can be found in all states east of the Rocky Mountains except the states bordering the Gulf Coast. The smallmouth bass likes a different type of habitat than the largemouth bass; it likes to live in clear, deep, rocky, cold water or in the rapid waters of streams and rivers.

Smallmouth bass are predators, just like their cousin the largemouth bass. The smallmouth bass feed on the same small animals as the largemouth bass, but they like baits that are smaller, such as small minnows, worms, crawfish, and some small bugs.

The Pike Family

The pike family is another group of fish that can be found in lakes around the United States. The most prevalent type of fish in this group is the muskellunge, or the muskie. Muskies can be found from southern Canada through Wisconsin, Michigan, Minnesota, Ohio, and New York; in the Susquehanna, Potomac, and Delaware river systems; and as far south as some of the waters in the Tennessee valley states. Muskies live in the clear, cool water of lakes, rivers, and flowages. The biggest muskie ever caught weighed sixty-nine pounds, fifteen ounces. Muskies feed on larger bait fish such as small trout, bass, or larger shiners.

The northern pike can be found in most of Canada and many areas of the northern United States as far west as the Continental Divide. Pike feed all year long. They are less active in the winter months and more active when the water warms in the springtime. Pike are like bass in that they live and feed around structures such as weeds, fallen trees, and rocks. Pike feed in daylight, mostly on smaller fish. Early morning is a good time to catch them because that's when they are hungry.

Another type of fish in the pike family is the pickerel. The pickerel is the smallest member of the pike family; eight- or nine-pound pickerel are the largest you will catch. Pickerel live in streams, lakes, and ponds in New England, New Jersey, and southern New York. Pickerel feed on the same small fish as the northern pike.

The Panfish

The smallest group of fish is the panfish. The panfish consist of bluegills, crappies, rock bass, sunfish, and yellow perch. Panfish are mostly caught for food. They can be found in the United States in over a million ponds, lakes, and reservoirs from coast to coast.

The key to catching panfish is to use small bait and to fish them very slowly. Worms—both red worms and meal-worms—are the best bait. The bluegill, also called bream or brim, swim in schools, and the bigger ones can be found around their nests in warmer, shallower waters. Their nests consist of clean gravel and sandy beds, and they are easily seen.

The crappies are members of the sunfish family and are a good fish to eat. Crappies can be found and caught in the same areas as the bluegill: in deep cover such as brush piles, docks, submerged or fallen trees, rock piles, and

boulders. Crappies love to feed on small minnows. The biggest crappie ever caught was five pounds, three ounces.

Rock bass are also called the goggle eye or red eye. The biggest of the rock bass is about twelve inches long. The rock bass prefer to live in the same areas as the smallmouth bass. This small fish will take almost any small food including but not limited to worms, crawfish, minnows, grasshoppers, and other insects and grubs. The best time to catch these fish is in the evening and at night.

Sunfish are probably one of the best known of the panfish. Sunfish are also called pumpkinseed. The fish have very small mouths, so small baits must be used. Sunfish live in the same waters as the bluegill. Because sunfish are easy to catch, they are a lot of fun for small children.

Yellow perch are fun to catch and delicious when freshly cooked. The biggest on record was approximately four pounds. Yellow perch are found mostly in lakes and ponds. They will eat almost any live bait you put in front of them. Small minnows will be your best bait since the yellow perch will feed most aggressively on them. Yellow perch can also be caught on small lures.

Trout

The final group of fish is the trout: brook trout, brown trout, and rainbow trout. The brook trout is found mostly in small

streams, but these fish also live in cold water ponds, lakes, and rivers. The biggest brook trout ever caught was fourteen pounds, eight ounces. Brook trout can be found in most cold regions of the United States, particularly in the northeastern states. These fish feed on shrimp, crawfish, and some other small organisms. They can also be caught with worms, small bugs, and other small lures, such as spinners and flies.

The brown trout originated in England. It averages about ten pounds in the United States. Large brown trout will eat almost anything, including birds, frogs, and mice, but the brown trout is essentially an insect-eating fish. Brown trout, also called sea trout, travel to the oceans, where the freshwater mixes with the saltwater.

The rainbow trout is considered one of the greatest game fish of the world. The rainbow trout that return from the saltwater sea are called steelheads. Rainbow trout are jumpers; when they are hooked they put on a great display of aerial acrobatics. Rainbow trout like streams' fast-moving waters. Like the other trout, rainbow trout feed on insects, but during some seasons of the year they will feed on larger baits, such as small fish, crawfish, or even freshwater shrimp.

Other Freshwater Fish
Some other fish that you may encounter while freshwater fishing are catfish, salmon, lake trout, eels, shad, and Dolly Varden.

Can I Eat the Fish I Catch?

All of these fish are edible, meaning you can eat them, but some fish may taste better than others. You also have to be careful of the small bones of the fish. When you catch a fish to bring home for dinner, give it to an adult to be properly cleaned, or filleted. Still, when you fillet and eat panfish or trout, which have been known to have a lot of small bones, it's often hard to clean out every little bone. Be careful and eat slowly so that you don't choke.

Fly-Fishing

Fly fishers tie to the end of their rods bait that is designed to imitate the live food of game fish—insects, minnows, and other natural foods. Fly-fishing can be done in either freshwater or saltwater. It is estimated that over a quarter of a million people pursue fly-fishing as a hobby.

Fly-fishing dates to the first or second century B.C. in Macedonia, where brown-trout anglers attached feathers to their hooks to imitate the insects in streams. The materials used today include fur, feathers, thread, tinsel, and wool.

There is a special art and skill required in casting a fly. This is so that the fly will look as if it is prey: an insect emerging from the stream or returning to it to lay eggs, or rising to the surface to split its outer skin and emerge with wings. Fly fishers will spend years perfecting their art. Fly-fishing is an excellent way to hone your athletic skill as well as learn how to move with ease and grace.

3 Saltwater Fishing

Saltwater is the type of water that we see in the oceans around the world. The reason this type of water is called saltwater is because the water has salt in it—if you taste the water you can taste the salt.

You can test the water you swim in at the beach by taking a paper plate, Frisbee, or even a bucket, putting ocean water in it, and letting it sit in the sun for about one hour. After an hour, when the water has disappeared, you should find salt. Many different species of fish live in saltwater, and most of them are a lot of fun to catch.

Where to Saltwater Fish

Saltwater is the type of water that makes up the seas, bays, and oceans of the world. If you live in a state that is on the coast of either the Atlantic Ocean, Pacific Ocean, or the Gulf of Mexico, you live within a short drive of some great fishing.

All of the following saltwater fishing spots are productive, meaning they are places where you can catch a lot of fish—maybe even a very big fish—if you are in the right place at the right time.

Fishing Structures

If you want to do some saltwater fishing near your home and you or your family do not have a boat or a house near a beach or bay there are some structures you can fish from:

* a pier—a large wooden structure built into a harbor and designed so that people can go out over the water
* a jetty—a structure of rocks which usually juts out from a beach and which is usually home to a lot of different fish
* a bridge—any structure that crosses over water

All of these structures can be fished from with ease. The main concern you should have is for your safety. When fishing from a man-made structure that juts out into or out over the bay or ocean, you must be especially careful. Stand clear of unprotected edges and never lean over a protective rail or rope.

Fishing Boats

If you do not have a bridge, pier, or jetty to fish off of near your home, you may live near a marina that is home to a public fishing boat or party boat. These boats are for hire—meaning you pay a small fee to fish on them. These boats will supply you with rods, reels, and bait. You will be fishing with a lot of other people on this kind of boat and

it could be crowded, but you have an opportunity to catch some nice fish.

If you do not want to fish on a crowded boat, you can fish from a charter boat. These boats are usually smaller and much more expensive to use. The advantages of a charter boat are that you can fish on a much less crowded boat, and the captain and first mate will usually fish for whatever catch you want, whereas on a party boat you are limited to what that particular boat is fishing for.

Fishing from the Beach: Surf Casting

The beach is the last place you can look to fish from if you do not have access to a boat or dock. Many big fish are caught right in the surf just off the beach.

Types of Saltwater Fish

There are thousands of different types of saltwater fish around the world. What follows are descriptions of the more popular fish groups.

Marlin

The first group of salt-water fish is the marlin. The marlin is one of the most popular game fish in the world. Marlins are not very tasty, so they are caught not so much for food as for the challenge—they put up a tremendous fight and make dramatic jumps when they are hooked.

There are a few types of marlin. From the largest to the small-est, they are the black marlin, blue marlin, striped marlin, and white marlin. The mar-lin has a bill on the front of its body, and for that reason it is sometimes called a bill-fish. Marlins feed on very large baits, such as tuna, mahimahi (dolphinfish), and jacks.

The marlin is not the only game fish that has a bill. Other fish that have bills and are chased by fishermen are the sailfish, which is a tremendous jumper and a very pretty fish; the swordfish, which is the tastiest of the billfish (and the strongest, pound for pound); and the spearfish, which has the shortest bill.

Tuna

Tuna are chased for food rather than for their fight, although they are among the toughest fighting fish of the oceans. Tuna are found all over the world in both cold and warm waters. There are several different types of tuna.

From the biggest to the smallest, they are:

* the bluefin tuna, which can grow to over one thousand pounds
* the bigeye tuna, which is extremely tasty and is eaten by the Japanese as sushi
* the yellowfin tuna, which is the prettiest of the tuna and one of the tastiest
* the longfin albacore, which is the type of tuna you get in the cans of tuna you buy at the grocery
* the blackfin tuna, which is found mostly in the warmer areas of the world

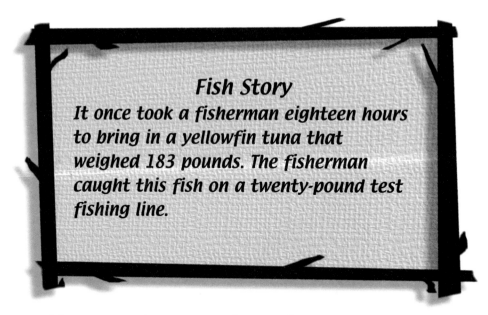

Fish Story
It once took a fisherman eighteen hours to bring in a yellowfin tuna that weighed 183 pounds. The fisherman caught this fish on a twenty-pound test fishing line.

There are a few types of tuna that are not as tasty as the others. These tuna are the skipjack tuna, false albacore, green bonito, and Atlantic bonito, all significantly smaller than the rest. Tuna usually roam the deep parts of the oceans searching for large schools of squid, mackerel, herring, and other small fish. They can be caught by trolling, which means to pull either lures or fresh bait at a fixed speed behind the boat from which you are fishing.

Sharks

The sharks of the world are hunted by most, if not all, fishermen at one time or another in their fishing careers. The most popular sharks to catch are the great white shark, which is the largest of the predator sharks and the most feared; the mako shark, which is the shark most targeted for its great fight and  for its great taste; the thresher shark, which has the longest tail of all sharks and is good to eat; the tiger shark, which is probably the most deadly of the sharks; and the hammerhead shark, which is the most ferocious and most feared by divers and swimmers because it is known to roam shallow waters.

There are too many sharks to name, but these sharks are the most popular among fishermen. Some other sharks that are targeted by fishermen are the blacktip shark, bull shark, blue shark, reef shark, brown shark, and dusky shark.

All of these sharks give a dramatic fight when hooked, but they should not be killed just for that. Most of them are inedible; so if you do catch a shark someday, let it go if you do not plan to eat it.

Double Trouble

A free diver (a diver without scuba gear) once speared a hammerhead shark weighing 1,600 pounds. The shark was fifteen feet long. When fishermen cut the shark open, they found half of another type of shark, with an estimated weight of 110 pounds!

Shark Attack!

Don't worry—chances are, it won't happen. However, if it does . . .

There are about three hundred documented cases of shark attacks each year worldwide. The great white shark attacks generally because it confuses humans with its usual food, seals and sea lions. The bull shark, on the other hand, will attack a human for no reason.

Although the odds of your being attacked by a shark are remote—while swimming or diving, you are 1,000 times more likely to drown than to be attacked by a shark—it is wise to take precautions.

* Don't swim or dive in areas where sharks are common.
* Don't go in the water where others are fishing.
* When swimming, swim with others and avoid swimming at dusk or after dark. (This is when sharks feed and swim closer to shore.)
* Do not enter the water if you see large numbers of fish or if fish are acting strangely.

Bottom Fish

Bottom fish are the fish that roam the bottom of the sea near sunken ships, rock piles, or ledges. The following are some of the most popular with fishermen: the blackfish, which is good to eat and can be found around structures in colder waters; the

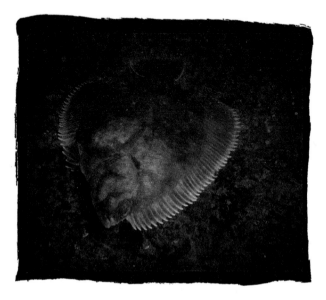

sea bass, which can be eaten and is very abundant around structures and sometimes in open bottom; the flounder, which is found in muddy bottom and feeds on small organisms; the summer flounder, which looks similar to the flounder but is more aggressive and feeds on small fish, shrimp, and crabs; and the cod, which roams the bottom of the ocean looking for wrecks. There are a tremendous number of bottom fish all over the world. The more popular ones live in the northeastern waters of the Atlantic Ocean.

Striped Bass

The striped bass is a fantastic game fish. It is fun to catch, and most fishermen will do almost anything to catch one of these trophy fish, no matter what their size. The striped bass got its name because of the stripes that run down the side of its body. The striped bass feeds on most bottom-dwelling fish, including the ones mentioned above. It also feeds on eels, bunker, herring, and some crabs. The striped bass can be caught with lures, live bait, and even some dead cut bait (pieces of dead fish used as bait).

The largest striped bass weigh fifty pounds or more. People catch striped bass from boats, the beach, piers, jetties, docks, and even from the tops of bridges. If you ever get the chance to catch one of these great game fish, it will be a proud accomplishment.

Bluefish

The bluefish, like the striped bass, feeds on most smaller fish it comes across. The bluefish got its name because of its blue back. Bluefish are a very aggressive fish with extremely sharp teeth that can cut through another fish like a hot knife through butter. Bluefish are not a great eating fish; their meat tends to be a little oily.

Bluefish can be caught on almost anything you put at the end of your fishing rod if the bluefish are in a feeding frenzy. In the northeastern part of the United States, bluefish are often very abundant and can be seen feeding on the surface of bays and the ocean. The small baby bluefish are called snappers, and when the water gets warm, they can be caught off most beaches, piers, and docks.

Weakfish

The weakfish gets its name because of its weak jaw. When hooked, the mouth of the weakfish has a tendency to tear if too much pressure is put on it. Weakfish feed on all of the same fish as bluefish and striped bass, but they can sometimes be more aggressive than bluefish and bass. At other times, they are not aggressive at all. Weakfish like the same living conditions as bluefish and striped bass, which is warm water and areas with a lot of bait.

The weakfish is very tasty and is very pretty when just taken out of the water. The weakfish is also called the sea trout because it can have a color pattern similar to that of its cousin, the freshwater brown trout.

Other Saltwater Fish

Some other saltwater fish that you may encounter while fishing the northeastern United States are the blowfish, which has a tendency to fill up with air or water when touched (they do this as a safety mechanism against predators); the porgy, which is a small fish that roams close to the bottom and can be very tasty; the kingfish, which is a bottom fish that is small and very tasty as well; and the sea robin, which is considered by many to be a junk fish, but which has wings like a bird.

4 Fishing Equipment

Now that you have an overview of what fish you might be able to catch, it's time to take a closer look at setting up your equipment.

Fishing Rods

The first thing you need is a fishing rod. A fishing rod can be made out of several different materials: wood (such as a long stick you might find in your backyard); a bamboo pole, which can be found at

your local tackle shop or fishing store; or a fiberglass or graphite fishing rod, which you can buy from a fishing store or your local sports store.

Today most fishermen fish with a rod that is made of either fiberglass or graphite. Both of these materials provide a very delicate feel and the strength needed to bring in that big fish when it comes along. These rods come in all different sizes, and they range in price from a couple of dollars to hundreds of dollars, depending on the quality of the materials used and the level of workmanship involved. A fishing rod consists of grips, a reel seat (where the fishing reel is placed on the rod), and fishing guides for the fishing line to go through.

There are two types of fishing rods. One type is a spinning fishing rod, which has extra big guides for the fishing line to go through. The guides are extra big so that the line can pass through the guides with very little resistance when casting. The other type of fishing rod is the conventional fishing rod. This rod is used mostly when fishing from a boat, so they are sometimes called boat rods. This rod has smaller guides to keep the fishing line on top of the rod since this type of fishing rod is held with the guides and reel on top of the rod.

Fishing Reels

With a fiberglass or graphite fishing rod, you will need a fishing reel. A fishing reel can be found in the store where you find your fishing rod. Fishing reels come in different styles, types, and sizes.

One type of fishing reel is a spinning reel. This type of reel is used for casting lures and baits out a distance from where you are. The spinning reel is simple to use and can be used in both fresh-water and saltwater fishing. The advantage of a spinning reel is that you can cast whatever you are using to catch fish out to where the fish may be with little effort. The spinning reel will be under-neath the fishing rod

when the fishing rod is being held.

Another type of reel is a conventional reel. This type of reel can also be used for casting, but it is usually used on a con-ventional fishing rod, which is used for fishing with bait and some lures. When using a conventional fishing rod and reel, if the rod is being held by the fisherman, the reel will be on top of the fishing rod, not underneath as a spinning reel would be.

Both of these types of reels are sold in fishing or sports equipment stores. If you have any further questions about these fishing reels, just ask someone in the fishing store or sporting equipment store; they will assist you and guide you to what you are looking for.

Fishing Line

If you are fishing with a bamboo pole or wooden stick, you do not need a fishing reel; all you need is fishing line. Fishing line can be found in your local fishing supply store. If you are using a fiberglass or graphite rod, fishing line is used on your reel and is the connection from your fishing rod and reel to the hook and bait. There are all different sizes and colors of fishing line. Usually the smaller the fish, the lighter the fishing line, and vice versa. The most common type of fishing line is monofilament. This type of fishing line is almost transparent, so the fish don't see it in the water. You can buy monofilament fishing line with different line strengths, meaning if the line has a ten-pound test rating, in theory the line will break when ten pounds of pressure is put onto it. The pound test rating can range from a one-pound test to a four hundred–pound test.

The other type of fishing line is a braided fishing line. Braided fishing line is just that—a line made of small fibers that are braided together to make one solid fishing line. The braided lines are stronger and thinner than the monofilament, and, unlike the monofilament, the braided fishing line will not stretch. You must be very careful when using braided fishing line because if it rubs against you, it can easily cut you.

Hooks, Sinkers, and Floats

After you have your fishing line, you will need hooks, swivels, sinkers, and floats to attach to the end of it. These items are called terminal tackle. The hook is attached to the very end of your fishing line, and hooks come in many shapes and sizes. The type of hook you use depends on the type of fish you are trying to catch and the type of bait you are using.

As you move from the hook back along your line to your fishing rod, you may attach a sinker. A sinker is a piece of metal, usually lead, that is attached to your fishing line to sink the hook and bait to the bottom of the water. Sinkers, like hooks, come in different sizes with weights ranging from less than an ounce to over a pound. The weight of the sinker you use depends on the fishing conditions. If the water is deep or fast moving, you will use a heavier sinker, but if the water is shallow or still, you may choose not to use a weight or to use only a very light weight.

If you want to keep your bait off the bottom of the water, you will use a float; if you want your bait on the bottom of the water, you will use only a sinker. Floats, like everything else we have discussed, come in different shapes and sizes. If you are fishing with a heavy bait or in rough water, you may want to use a float that is bigger than normal. If you are using a light bait, or fishing in calm waters, your float may not have to be so big. Floats are used not only to keep your bait off the bottom but also as strike indicators. If a fish hits your bait, the float will move in a funny way, or slip under the water, telling you that you have a fish.

Lures

Instead of using bait to catch fish, you can use a fake bait, or a lure. Lures are made to resemble most bait fish. A lure is usually cast out and retrieved by the fisherman. While being retrieved, the lure will resemble an injured bait fish and, hopefully, the fish will think that it is real.

Fishing lures come in thousands of colors, shapes, sizes, and materials. Lures are used in all types of fishing, from fishing for small trout in streams to trying to catch that one thousand–pound marlin in a thousand feet of water in the

middle of the ocean. In any given situation, some lures will work better than others. That is why there are so many lures to choose from.

The best advice to follow when choosing a lure is buy the lure that the guy in the fishing store says to buy! The guy in the fishing store will probably know better than anyone which lures will catch the most fish because he knows which kinds have been working on the local fish and which have not.

Saltwater Tackle

When it comes to fishing tackle for saltwater fishing, all the same principles apply. The only difference is that your rods, your reels, your hooks, and your sinkers and floats will probably get bigger, and your line will probably get stronger, all depending on what you are fishing for.

In bodies of saltwater, such as bays and oceans, your fishing gear will vary in size, depending on the type of fishing you are doing. If you are shark fishing, you will use very big fishing rods and fishing reels. If you are bottom fishing, you will use fishing rods and fishing reels similar to those you would use if you were freshwater fishing. The type and size of fishing rod and fishing reel you use depend on what you are fishing for, where you will be fishing, and how you will be fishing.

5 Issues Surrounding Fishing

In the fishing world today, there is controversy between commercial fishermen (fishermen who catch fish to sell them) and recreational fishermen (people who, like most of us, fish for sport). The controversy is over fishing rights: rights to catch certain fish species and rights to fish in specific areas of the ocean. Today there are many fish shortages—meaning that there are not as many fish in the oceans as there used to be—because of overfishing by

both commercial and recreational fishermen. Because there is a shortage of fish, both commercial fishermen and recreational fishermen are restricted by the government from fishing for certain species. As a result, commercial fishermen and recreational fishermen are often at odds.

Recreational fishermen tend to feel that commercial fishermen are depleting the amount of fish in the ocean. Commercial fishermen tend to feel that they have every right to fish for any species that recreational fishermen can fish for. This is why, when it comes to regulating who can fish for a specific species (and the amount of fish a fisherman can keep), recreational fishermen and commercial fishermen do not see eye-to-eye.

The issues dividing commercial fishermen and recreational fishermen are difficult to resolve, so all the government can do is try to work out a compromise good enough to keep both groups happy. The government does this by giving each group of fishermen rights to certain fish species and certain fishing grounds.

Issues of Overfishing the Oceans

The issues between commercial fishermen and recreational fishermen are not the only issues that exist among the fishermen of the world. There are the larger issues of which country has the right to fish specific areas of the oceans. Each country has possession of the 200 miles of ocean that border its coastline, and each country can regulate the fishing that goes on within those areas.

Controversy begins when one country's fishermen start to fish inside the 200 miles of water surrounding the coastline of another country. When a country fishes in another country's waters without that country's permission, legal issues regarding who can fish where arise.

The only way countries can resolve their differences is in the world court system. In this court system, the laws are applied to the facts, and controversies that exist over fishing rights are resolved with an enforceable decision.

Laws to Regulate Fishing

As a result of the issues that have come up about fishing in this country, state and federal governments have written laws to regulate fishing and the size of fish that can be kept by both commercial and recreational fishermen. These laws are designed to prevent the depletion of certain fish species. These laws are upheld by local, state, and federal law enforcement agencies that check on both commercial and recreational fishermen. "Checking" usually involves representatives from enforcement agencies boarding boats or meeting boats at their docks and checking the size and amount of fish the fishermen have caught. If the laws have been violated by the fishermen, they are fined; because they have

broken the law, they have to pay a large sum of money to the government.

Every year the laws change. It is your job and the job of other fishermen to learn the laws so that you do not violate them. You can find a copy of these laws at your local fishing store or at a law enforcement agency in your area.

Aquaculture: The Raising and Harvesting of Fish

Because the world's oceans are being depleted by fishermen, many businesses are starting to raise fish in very large fish tanks. The raising of fish in tanks to sell to fish markets is called aquaculture. What aquaculture does for the fish food industry is truly amazing. First, it takes pressure off the migrating fish stocks of the oceans of the world. Without such pressure on certain fish species, those species are able to grow; maybe in the future they will no longer be considered a depleted fish stock.

There are specific types of fish that are raised in tanks to be sold in fish markets. Those fish include the catfish, striped bass, salmon, and trout.

The Competition: Freshwater and Saltwater Fishing Tournaments

Have you ever watched television and seen a fishing show?

Most likely, the host of that show is a professional fisherman. A professional fisherman is a person who fishes in fishing tournaments—sometimes for lots of money! Usually these tournaments are won by the fisherman or fishermen who catch the biggest fish.

There are many different types of fishing tournaments held throughout the world. Sometimes the first prize in a fishing tournament can be as much as $300,000. Largemouth bass fishing tournaments are probably the most popular type of fishing tournament in the United States today. In a

largemouth bass tournament, a professional fisherman and
an amateur fisherman usually fish together on the same
boat. The professional fisherman is limited to five fish, and
the goal for each fisherman is to catch the biggest five fish he
or she can by the end of the day. This goes on for two or three

days. At the end of the tournament, the fisherman with the fish that, when taken all together, weigh the most, wins the tournament and takes the prize money.

There are also marlin tournaments. During these tournaments, large sport fishing boats with about four or five fishermen on board go out and try to catch the biggest marlin. These tournaments are usually at least two days long, and sometimes the winning fish can weigh up to one thousand pounds.

Shark tournaments are another very popular fishing tournament. In these tournaments, a large number of boats go out for a day, and whichever boat comes back with the largest shark wins a large sum of money.

Other types of tournaments are local fishing tournaments for local fish. These tournaments are not as popular as the other tournaments we have discussed because they don't pay out as much money.

The big problem with these fishing tournaments is the unnecessary killing of fish. The goal of every fisherman in these tournaments is to catch the biggest fish; and since they don't know if they have the biggest fish until they get back to the dock, they have a tendency to kill most of the big fish that they catch. You should take this into consideration before you decide to participate in a tournament.

6 Safety

Your single most important concern when you go out fishing on a boat should be safety. A boat can be a very dangerous thing if you do not take the proper precautions. Before going out on a fishing boat, make a safety check. The following safety items should be on board:

* a life preserver for every person who will be on the boat, plus a throwable flotation device
* a noise-making device, such as a whistle or a horn
* a set of flares or a flare gun
* a first-aid kit

When you are on the boat you should wear your life preserver at all times unless an adult on board the boat with you says it is okay for you not to wear it. Always avoid standing up when the boat is in motion—since you might fall off if the boat hits a wave. Finally, you should make sure that all of the equipment you bring on the boat is stored safely so that it won't fall overboard or slide all over the boat and injure someone .

Fishing Safety

Fishing can be fun if you do it safely. There are a lot of things that you must remember when handling fishing equipment. Fishing hooks can be very dangerous if not handled properly.

One of the key things to remember when handling fishing hooks is that you should always handle them by the shank of the hook. If you do not handle the hook by the shank, you risk the chance of getting the point of the hook caught in your hand or some other part of your body.

When storing hooks in your tackle box or on your fishing rod, remember to put either a small cork or a piece of foam on the point. That way, if you happen to grab the fishing rod or put your hand in the tackle box without looking, you will not get a hook stuck in your hand.

Fishing knives are another dangerous fishing tool. To prevent cutting yourself when handling a fishing knife, always remember to hold the knife by its handle and not by its blade. Also, when you are storing the fishing knife, always put the knife into a protective holder to avoid damaging yourself or anything you may have in your tackle box. Always ask an adult or parent how to use a fishing knife before handling it.

Fishing line can also be very dangerous if not handled the right way. If you get tangled in the fishing line, you can cut yourself or even stop the blood flow from one part of your body to another. Talk to someone at your local tackle shop for proper instruction on handling line.

In conclusion, fishing can be a great sport if you do it safely and smartly. If you want to go out and try and catch a fish in a pond, lake, bay, or ocean, remember that the more you know, the more successful you will be. To all of you, the best of luck in your fishing adventures!

Glossary

Amateur
A person who participates in a sport but does not get paid.

Bill
The part of a marlin, sailfish, or swordfish that sticks out from its face. These fish use their bill to hurt the fish they are going to eat.

Conventional
A fishing rod or reel that is not a spinning reel or fly reel.

Dead cut
Bait chunks of dead fish that are put on a fishing hook to catch other fish.

Flare
Device that lights up so brightly that people can see it from very long distances. Flares are used to tell other people that you need help.

Grip
The part of the fishing rod that you hold on to.

Grub
A small insect used for bait.

Guides
The part of the fishing rod that the line is put through so it can go from the reel to the tip of the rod.

Herring
A small bait fish that roams the colder waters of oceans and bays. Larger fish love to feed on herring.

Jetty
A line of large rocks that extends into a sea, lake, or river to protect the shore from erosion.

Ledge
An underwater ridge or reef, especially near the shore.

Life Preserver
A device that floats and that you put on like a jacket to keep from drowning.

Live Bait
Live fish that is put on a hook and then back into the water to catch bigger fish.

Monofilament
An opaque material that is used to make a fishing line.

Pier
Wooden structure that is built out over the water so people can fish more easily and in deeper water.

Predator
An animal that kills and eats other animals.

Reel Seat
The part of a fishing rod where the fishing reel is attached and tightened so that it does not fall off the rod.

Reservoir
A body of water, made by man, where water is stored for irrigation or drinking.

Shank
The long part of a fish hook that acts like a backbone to the rest of the hook.

Terminal Tackle
The hooks, sinkers, floats, and lures that you put at the end of your fishing line.

Resources

In the United States

National Park Service (NPS)
1849 C Street NW
Washington, DC 20240
(202) 208-6843
Web site: http://www.nps.gov

Sierra Club
85 Second Street, Second Floor
San Francisco, CA 94105
(415) 977-5500
Web site: http://www.sierraclub.org

In Canada

Canadian Parks and Wilderness Society (CPWS)
880 Wellington Street, Suite 506
Ottawa, ON K1R 6K7
(800) 333-WILD
Web site: http://www.cpaws.org

Web Sites

Fishfinder
http://thefishfinder.com/links/

Nor'east Saltwater Online
http:// www.noreast.com

Screaming Reel
http://www.screamingreel.com

Sporting Adventures Launchpad
http://www.spav.com/sa/basecamp/launchpad/default.htm

Movies

Jaws (Remember, though, this is only a fantasy flick—NOT reality!)
Man of Aran
The Old Man and the Sea
A River Runs Through It

Television Shows

Bass Masters (TNN)
Fishing with Orlando Wilson (TNN)
Jimmy Houston's Outdoors (ESPN)
Mark Sosin's Saltwater Journal (TNN)
North American Fisherman (ESPN)
The Spanish Fly (ESPN)
Walker's Lay Chronicles (ESPN)

Ask Around

Speak to someone who works in your local tackle shop or who has been fishing for many years.

For Further Reading

Bates, Joseph D., Jr. *Fishing.* New York: Random House, 1988.

Bauer, Erwin, et al. *The Saltwater Fisherman's Bible.* New York: Doubleday, 1991.

Goadby, Peter. *Saltwater Gamefishing: Offshore and Onshore* Camden, ME: International Marine Publishing Co., 1992.

Logue, Victoria, and Frank Logue. *Kids Outdoors: The Totally Nonboring Backcountry Skills Guide.* New York: McGraw-Hill, 1996.

Morey, Shaun. *Incredible Fishing Stories.* New York: Workman Publishing, 1994.

Samson, Jack. *The Sportsman's World.* New York: Holt, Rinehart & Winston, 1974. (This one is a bit old, but if you can find it in your library, it's a classic!)

Index

Credits

About the Author

Captain Dane Solomon started fishing when he was about two or three. His fishing knowledge comes from going out on the water and finding fish, reading books, and watching other, more experienced fishermen. He is a Fishing Charter Captain and has produced his own television show, *Fishing Long Island.* He really loves to teach young people how to fish.